T0321287

SHARK:

Apex Predator

FIRST EDITION

Series Editor Deborah Lock; **US Senior Editor** Shannon Beatty; **Editor** Radhika Haswani;
Senior Art Editor Ann Cannings; **Art Editor** Kanika Kalra; **Producer, Pre-Production** Nadine King;
Picture Researcher Sakshi Saluja; **DTP Designers** Neeraj Bhatia, Dheeraj Singh;
Managing Editor Soma Chowdhury; **Art Director** Martin Wilson;
Reading Consultant Linda Gambrell, PhD

THIS EDITION

Editorial Management by Oriel Square
Produced for DK by WonderLab Group LLC
Jennifer Emmett, Erica Green, Kate Hale, *Founders*

Editors Grace Hill Smith, Libby Romero, Michaela Weglinski;
Photography Editors Kelley Miller, Annette Kiesow, Nicole DiMella; **Managing Editor** Rachel Houghton;
Designers Project Design Company; **Researcher** Michelle Harris; **Copy Editor** Lori Merritt;
Indexer Connie Binder; **Proofreader** Larry Shea; **Reading Specialist** Dr. Jennifer Albro;
Curriculum Specialist Elaine Larson

Published in the United States by DK Publishing
1745 Broadway, 20th Floor, New York, NY 10019

Copyright © 2023 Dorling Kindersley Limited
DK, a Division of Penguin Random House LLC
23 24 25 26 10 9 8 7 6 5 4 3 2 1
001-334014-July/2023

A catalog record for this book
is available from the Library of Congress.
HC ISBN: 978-0-7440-7357-7
PB ISBN: 978-0-7440-7358-4

DK books are available at special discounts when purchased in bulk for sales promotions, premiums, fundraising, or educational use. For details, contact: DK Publishing Special Markets, 1745 Broadway, 20th Floor, New York, NY 10019
SpecialSales@dk.com

Printed and bound in China

The publisher would like to thank the following for their kind permission to reproduce their images:
a=above; c=center; b=below; l=left; r=right; t=top; b/g=background

123RF.com: solarseven 51tr; **Alamy Stock Photo:** ArteSub 33crb, BSIP SA / JACOPIN 35bc, Harry Collins 26-27bc, Chris Gomersall 43tr, Matt Heath 8-9br, Louise Murray 37b, 40tl, Nature Picture Library / 2020VISION / Alex Mustard 44-45bc, Nature Picture Library / Alex Mustard 42tl, Doug Perrine 31tr, 38tl, 38-39bc, Robertharding / Louise Murray 55tr, Marko Steffensen 42-43bc, 61cla, WaterFrame_fba 53tr, WaterFrame_tat 44clb; **Dreamstime.com:** Greg Amptman 12tl, Fiona Ayerst 22-23bc, 60tl, Nicolás Sánchez Biezma 14tl, Salvador Ceja 31crb, Csaba Fikker 6tl, Fototrips 18clb, Frhojdysz 6cl, Simone Gatterwe 49tr, Elizabeth Hoffmann 50tl, Izanbar 20br, Jagronick 61clb, Kelpfish 53bl, Torsten Kuenzlen 19cla, Yisi Li 18-19bc, Lukaves 34crb, 55cl, Shane Myers 13bl, Naluphoto 18tl, 21bl, 58-59bl, Photomailbox 56tl, Planetfelicity 36cb, 61tl, Ondřej Prosický 46tl, Radub85 26tl, Ramzes19846 54tl, Rixie 36tl, Michael Schmeling 13cr, Ian Scott 60cla, Sergioua 21tr, Akbar Solo 58tl, Starryvoyage 57tr, Syda Productions 45cra, Mogens Trolle 24tl, Michael Valos 32-33bc, 41cr, 51bl, Vkilikov 14clb, Vladvitek 34-35bc, 60bl, Martin Voeller 32tl, Dongfan Wang 32clb, Marcin Wojciechowski 39tr; **Getty Images:** Moment / by wildestanimal 52br; **Getty Images / iStock:** BartCo 46-47bc, Ryan Cake 30tl, Howard Chen 60clb, cinoby 17b, CoreyFord 7tr, Divepic 4-5, FionaAyerst 25tr, Michael Geyer 10-11, HakBak1979 14-15br, Hoatzinexp 24-25bc, June Jacobsen 22tl, LeicaFoto 54cr, Nature, food, landscape, travel 46clb, NNehring 44c, RainervonBrandis 27tr, Rebecca-Belleni-Photography 44tl, Natalie Robson 13tr, Philip Thurston 52tl, tswinner 16tl, vladoskan 49bl; **NASA:** EOSDIS / LANCE and GIBS / Worldview 59tr; **naturepl.com:** Franco Banfi 36br, Chris & Monique Fallows 48clb, Andy Murch 40-41bc, Doug Perrine 37tr; **Science Photo Library:** Roger Munns, Scubazoo 20tl, Louise Murray 48tl; **Shutterstock.com:** Michael Bogner 24bl, Willyam Bradberry 23t, frantisekhojdysz 6-7bc, Jessica Heim 28bl, Alessandro De Maddalena 30-31bc, Matt9122 10tl, 19tc, 33tt, shmatkov 51crb, Daniel Vasylyev 29t;

Cover images: *Front:* **Alamy Stock Photo:** Nature Picture Library / Chris & Monique Fallows;
Back: **Shutterstock.com:** Alex Vog clb; *Spine:* **Alamy Stock Photo:** Nature Picture Library / Chris & Monique Fallows b

All other images © Dorling Kindersley
For more information see: www.dkimages.com

For the curious
www.dk.com

Level
4

SHARK:
Apex Predator

Ruth A. Musgrave

CONTENTS

Predators of Predators
Young apex predators are prey to larger animals such as orca whales.

Shark Diet
A shark's diet varies depending on the species, the shark's age, and where it lives.

WHAT IS AN APEX PREDATOR?

An apex predator is more than the top dog, big boss, or scariest animal around. It sits at the top of a food web. It holds this spot because a healthy adult has few, if any, predators.

Large and in charge might describe apex predators. That's because apex predators tend to be big animals. Often, they hunt sizable prey and have extensive home ranges.

More than 500 kinds of sharks cruise the ocean and some freshwater rivers and lakes. They live in shallow water near the beach and in the middle of the ocean thousands of miles (km) away from shore. More than half live in the ocean's deeper depths. Though many sharks are top predators, not all sharks are apex predators.

Older Than Dinos
Sharks have existed for more than 400 million years. That's long before dinosaurs!

Food Web
A food web describes the overlap of all the food chains in a habitat.

What is the difference between a top predator and an apex predator? Scientists believe the presence of an apex predator causes a complex but positive chain reaction in a food web. Apex predators help maintain a healthy ecosystem.

Apex predators impact other animals by either eating them or scaring them away. The prey must find a balance between safety and finding enough food to eat. Without apex predators, the entire food web can be disrupted or even destroyed. A top predator, though important, might not have such an important or unique role.

Scientists are still learning which sharks throughout the world are apex predators. To do that, they must understand how animals in different food webs behave and how the animals use the habitat when sharks arrive and when they leave.

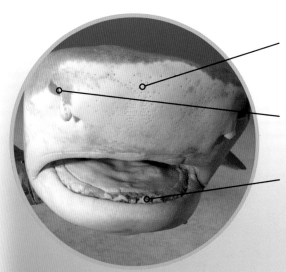

Ampullae of Lorenzini
Sensory pits help zero in on prey within the last few inches (cm) of a hunt.

Nostril
Up to two-thirds of a shark's brain is devoted to smell.

Teeth
Several rows of sharp teeth help catch, hold, and eat food.

Eyes
The tapetum lucidum in the back of the eyes works like mirrors to reflect light, helping a shark see in the dark.

Gill Slits
A shark breathes as water washes over gills and out gill slits.

Ears
A shark can hear something 800 feet (240 m) away.

Pectoral Fins
These are used to turn and stop and to provide lift.

SHARK ANATOMY

With super senses and powerful bodies, sharks are powerful predators.

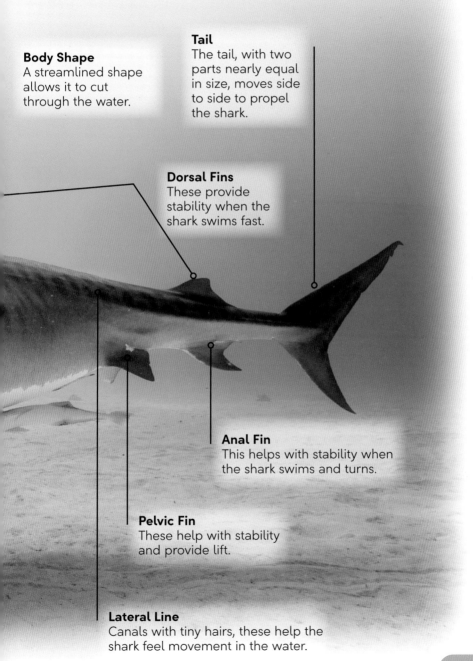

Body Shape
A streamlined shape allows it to cut through the water.

Tail
The tail, with two parts nearly equal in size, moves side to side to propel the shark.

Dorsal Fins
These provide stability when the shark swims fast.

Anal Fin
This helps with stability when the shark swims and turns.

Pelvic Fin
These help with stability and provide lift.

Lateral Line
Canals with tiny hairs, these help the shark feel movement in the water.

Traveling Tigers
Tiger sharks migrate long distances throughout the year to hunt in different habitats.

Solo Hunters
Tiger sharks sometimes hunt in the same areas with other tiger sharks, but they usually do not swim and hunt together.

TIGER SHARK

The tiger shark slowly swishes its tail back and forth as it swims through the shallow water in Shark Bay, Western Australia. Below the shark, seagrass meadows sway with the ocean currents.

The shark searches for sea turtles, sea snakes, seabirds, and dugongs at the water's surface. The streams of sunlight help reveal the prey's silhouettes. The tiger shark sees a green sea turtle and sneaks toward it. But the wary turtle turns, sees the shark, and quickly swims away. The tiger shark does not pursue the turtle. It is easier to catch unsuspecting prey.

The shark sees a cormorant snatch a fish. The diving seabird is too far away to catch. The shark changes its approach and swims toward the seafloor. A dolphin notices the predator on the hunt and swiftly swims into deeper water.

The dolphin won't find as much good food farther down, but it will be less likely to encounter a tiger shark there. Nearby, a startled dugong follows the dolphin's example and quickly swims to the less desirable seagrass in deeper water. A sea snake hunkers down in the seagrass to avoid detection, and then swims away.

Massive Meadow
Shark Bay, Western Australia, is home to one of the world's largest seagrass meadows.

Shark Bay
Shark Bay is an 8,500-square-mile (22,000-sq-km) refuge in Western Australia. That's a little bigger than Massachusetts, USA.

Protecting the Pod

Dolphins swim in small groups called pods. Traveling in pods helps protect dolphins from sharks, dolphins' main predator.

Dugongs

A dugong is a marine mammal found in warm coastal waters in the Indian and western Pacific Oceans.

The shark continues its search for a meal. It swims close to the ocean floor. Seagrass tickles its belly. Its faintly striped skin blends in with the light and shadows. This camouflage makes the 18-foot (5.5-m)-long fish hard to see, even in the sunny meadow. Ahead, it spots a stingray. The shark sneaks closer and closer. Then, in a burst of speed, the shark captures it.

Tiger sharks return to these seagrass meadows in the summer. They arrive then because more sea turtles, dolphins, sea snakes, and dugongs are in the area to follow their own prey or to breed.

Winter Trip
Many tiger sharks leave Shark Bay for the winter and travel in different directions. Some travel to different parts of Western Australia. One shark that scientists observed traveled all the way to South Africa.

Sea Snakes
Six species of sea snakes live in Shark Bay. Sea snakes are born in the water and spend their entire lives in the sea.

Fangs
Most sea snakes hunt fish. They paralyze their prey with their venomous fangs.

The presence of tiger sharks in Shark Bay is a great example of how an apex predator impacts an entire food web.

When more tiger sharks appear in the summer, the prey is forced to change its behavior. Some animals, like dolphins and dugongs, move from shallow water to safer, deeper water where the sharks hunt less often. Other animals, like sea snakes, hide in seagrass growing in shallow water but choose areas that the sharks visit less frequently because prey is less abundant.

The sharks' arrival to the seagrass meadow impacts other parts of the food web, too, changing which animal eats what and where. For example, when dolphins move to deeper water, the fish they hunted in shallow water get a break from their hungry predators. Seagrass gets a chance to grow when the dugongs graze elsewhere.

Shark Bay has provided a unique and important location to study how apex predators like tiger sharks interact with their habitat.

Sea Cows
Dugongs are called sea cows because they graze on seagrass, just like cows graze on grass. Dugongs pull up seagrass with their strong upper lips.

Tiger Stripes
Young tiger sharks have stripes, just like the animal they are named for. These stripes fade as the sharks get older.

Tiger sharks have a reputation for eating just about anything. Some have even been found with license plates and tires in their stomachs! They eat many things. But, like all sharks, they do not eat all the time or eat everything they see.

A tiger shark's many rows of serrated teeth help it slice through turtle shells and large animals like stingrays, sea lions, and octopuses.

Rough Landing
Every summer for about three weeks, tiger sharks gather near the coast of Hawaii. They wait for young albatrosses that are just learning to fly to rest on the ocean's surface.

Loggerhead Turtle

Toothy
Sharks lose teeth as they eat. A tooth from the row behind then moves up, and a new tooth grows in the back row.

Breathe Fast
Scientists attached cameras to loggerhead and green sea turtles to find out why tiger sharks eat loggerheads five times more often than green sea turtles. The footage shows that loggerheads spend more time at the water's surface, which might make them more visible. Green sea turtles take a quick breath and then dive.

19

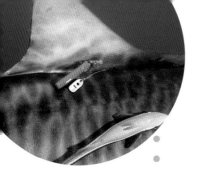

Shark Cam
Small cameras temporarily attached to tiger sharks and other sharks help give scientists an inside look at shark behavior, such as where these predators travel and how they interact with other animals.

Shark Tags
Between 1980 and 2018, scientists tagged more than 8,700 tiger sharks.

As they hunt, tiger sharks swim up and down from the water's surface to deeper water. Scientists call this a bounce dive or yo-yo technique. This hunting style might help them find prey in different places. Plus, it makes the shark less predictable to its prey.

Tiger sharks depend on the element of surprise. They stalk their prey to get as close as possible. Then, they use a quick burst of speed to catch it. If the prey sees the shark too soon and tries to escape, the shark often gives up the chase.

A tiger shark's movement, hunting style, and food preferences vary depending on what prey are available. They also vary depending on the age or size of the tiger shark.

Perfect Temperature
Tiger sharks, like many other sharks, prefer certain water temperatures. They travel throughout the year to find warmer or cooler water. Tiger sharks favor water temperatures between about 78°F and 82°F (25.5°C to 27.7°C).

Taking a Breath
Sharks use their nostrils to smell, not breathe.

Warm Water
This apex predator lives in warm, shallow waters along coasts around the world.

BULL SHARK

The lone bull shark cruises slowly through the murky water near the shore. Sand churned up by the rolling waves makes it nearly impossible to see through the water. The shark relies on its amazing sense of smell to find food. The water washes over its nostrils. The shark follows the scent of a smaller shark. Once the bull shark is close enough, it zooms quickly after its prey. First, it bumps the smaller shark with its blunt snout. Then, it bites down with its sharp teeth.

Following Smells

Scents travel a long way as ocean currents push them through the water. Think of a current as a stream or river within the sea. Sharks use currents to find prey that is far away.

Seeking Scents

Sharks swing their heads from side to side as they swim. This motion allows them to pick up scents from a bigger section of the ocean.

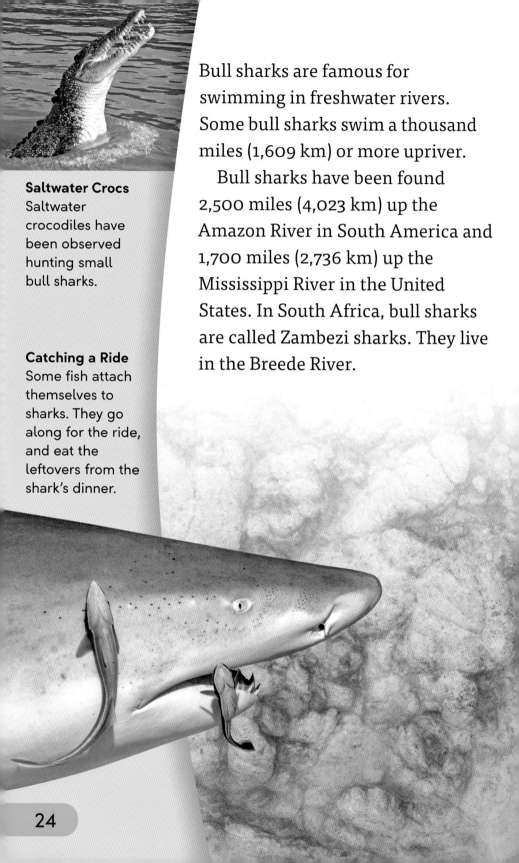

Saltwater Crocs
Saltwater crocodiles have been observed hunting small bull sharks.

Catching a Ride
Some fish attach themselves to sharks. They go along for the ride, and eat the leftovers from the shark's dinner.

Bull sharks are famous for swimming in freshwater rivers. Some bull sharks swim a thousand miles (1,609 km) or more upriver.

Bull sharks have been found 2,500 miles (4,023 km) up the Amazon River in South America and 1,700 miles (2,736 km) up the Mississippi River in the United States. In South Africa, bull sharks are called Zambezi sharks. They live in the Breede River.

Being able to move between saltwater and freshwater is rare. Usually, a freshwater animal cannot survive in saltwater, and a saltwater animal cannot survive in fresh water. Their kidneys, eyes, skin, and other body parts are designed for one type of water or the other.

But a bull shark can switch between the two environments. It is an amazing example of the adaptability of this apex predator.

Balancing Act
A bull shark's kidneys and liver help maintain the right balance of salt in its body.

My Space or Yours?
Bull sharks, tiger sharks, and great white sharks are considered the most dangerous sharks to humans. They do not hunt people. But where they hunt sometimes overlaps with where people play at the beach.

Female bull sharks often give birth in estuaries. An estuary is where a river and an ocean meet. It has a mix of saltwater and freshwater. Like all sharks, newborn bull sharks are born with teeth, and they are ready to hunt. And like all shark babies, the pups must fend for themselves. The tiny sharks make an excellent meal for a bigger animal. Estuaries and rivers provide a safer place for babies and young bull sharks to grow up, away from larger predators.

Bull sharks travel and eat alone. Depending on where they live, bull sharks eat a wide variety of prey. Fish, shrimp, crabs, squid, snails, sea stars, sea urchins, sea turtles, seabirds, other sharks, dolphins, and other marine mammals are all on their menu!

Bump and Bite
Because they often hunt in murky water, bull sharks bump and bite prey first to see if it would make a tasty meal.

Baby Bulls
Newborn bull sharks are some 30 inches (75 cm) long. That's about as long as a one-year-old human.

Adapting
When food is hard to find, bull sharks can slow down their metabolism so they need to eat less.

SHORTFIN MAKO SHARK

The brilliant blue mako shark races after its prey. Its pointed nose and sleek shape cut through the sea. Water rolls over its scales. The shark races up to the prey like a torpedo, grabs it with needle-like teeth, and then swallows it whole.

From nose to tail, a mako's body is one amazing adaptation after another. It's like taking all the best shark adaptations and then supercharging them to create a finely tuned race car.

The swiftest shark in the sea, the mako is built for speed. This powerful fish races up to 35 miles per hour (56 kph) and can leap 20 feet (6 m) into the air. Makos hunt fast-swimming food like tuna.

Unlike some sharks, mako sharks must keep swimming to breathe.

Their razor-sharp teeth easily slice through the flesh and bones of larger prey, such as swordfish, marlin, and dolphins.

The mako's tail propels it forward. The shark's loosely connected scales raise and lower to reduce drag in the water.

Even the mako's coloration shines like a race car. The shark's back ranges in color from brilliant blue to purple. Its sides are silvery, and its belly is a lighter shade of silver. This makes the shark disappear in the water—no matter if the prey is above, below, or beside the mako.

Short and Long
There are two kinds of mako sharks, the shortfin and the longfin.

Red and White Muscles

Makos, like other animals, have both red and white muscles. Though similar, white muscles are made of fibers that tire more quickly, and red muscles are made of fibers that tire less quickly.

Look under the hood of this race-car-like shark to find one more secret to its speed. Mako sharks are warm-blooded. Most sharks and other fish are cold-blooded. That means their body is the same temperature as the water around them. A mako shark's temperature is a few degrees higher than the surrounding seawater.

The mako shark's body retains heat rather than losing it. Its muscles are always warm. This means the shark can take off at top speed instantly.

Red muscles inside the mako's body help trap heat. They get warm when they are used. Because makos swim all the time, their red muscles are always warm. These muscles also warm the blood that is circulated throughout the rest of the body. This helps the shark maintain a higher body temperature.

Warm-Blooded Sharks
Great whites (above), porbeagle sharks, salmon sharks, and longfin makos are also warm-blooded.

Fishing for Makos
Makos are fished for their meat and fins. Their speed, power, size, and acrobatics also make them prized by recreational fishers.

Mouth Underneath

A hammerhead's mouth is on the underside of its body, which might make it easier to grab prey in the sand.

GREAT HAMMERHEAD SHARK

The great hammerhead swims along the ocean floor. It swings its head back and forth to search for animals buried in the sand. A stingray beneath the sand twitches its muscles. The hammerhead senses the hidden ray's movement. The ray stirs up a flurry of sand as it tries to escape its hiding place. But the big shark is fast.

Skates

A skate is related to both sharks and stingrays. It has a flat body and hides in the sand.

It uses its head to pin the ray to the seafloor. Then, while holding the ray down, the shark grabs it with its mouth.

This apex predator hunts and lives in coastal ecosystems. It preys on many animals found on the seafloor, such as smaller sharks, fish, squid, octopus, and crabs. But its favorite foods are rays and skates.

Head Shape
The great hammerhead is the largest of the nine species of hammerhead sharks. It can be identified by the shape of its head.

Little Shark
Newborn scalloped hammerhead sharks are 15 to 18 inches (38 to 45 cm) long, about the size of a loaf of bread.

Long-Distance Sense
Great hammerheads use the same sense to find their way hundreds of miles across the ocean and back again. They migrate toward warmer waters near the equator in the winter and toward cooler waters near the poles in the summer. They migrate to find food, give birth, or find mates.

A hammerhead shark uses its head for many things, including bumping and pinning its food. Like all sharks, sensory pits cover the hammerhead's head. These pits detect electrical currents given off when animals move their muscles. The shark's long, rectangular head provides more space for these sensory pits. This helps the hammerhead detect prey that's completely covered in sand.

Hammerhead sharks live in tropical and subtropical waters around the world.

With an eye located on both sides of its head, this shark has a three-dimensional view of the ocean. That means it can see all around—including above and below—at the same time. The location of its eyes also gives the shark excellent depth perception. You use depth perception to track and catch a ball. The shark needs it to track and catch moving prey.

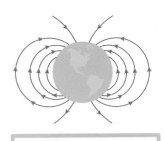

Magnetic Attraction
Earth has a magnetic field created by metals like iron in its molten core. Sensory pits called ampullae of Lorenzini allow sharks to detect changes in this magnetic field to tell which direction they are traveling.

ampullae of Lorenzini

Catch a Breath
Harbor seals come up for air about once every 30 minutes. They also haul out, or rest, on rocks, beaches, and drifting ice to escape from predators.

GREENLAND SHARK

The Greenland shark swims slowly and silently far below the polar ice. The giant shark's dark coloration helps it blend into the darker depths. The shark stalks a seal, secretly following it toward the water's surface. The seal swims toward a hole in the ice to catch a breath of air. The shark follows. Will the shark grab the seal then? Or will it wait until the seal is asleep in the water? Either way, the seal will not know the giant fish is there until it is too late.

Big Fish
The Greenland shark is the largest fish in the Arctic.

One word describes this apex predator: stealthy. Greenland sharks are as long as or slightly longer than a large great white shark. But while great whites use speed, Greenland sharks rely on slyness and an amazing ability to sneak up on prey.

Sharp Scales
Scientists must be cautious when handling a Greenland shark. Its sharp scales can cut their hands and rip through their thick diving suits.

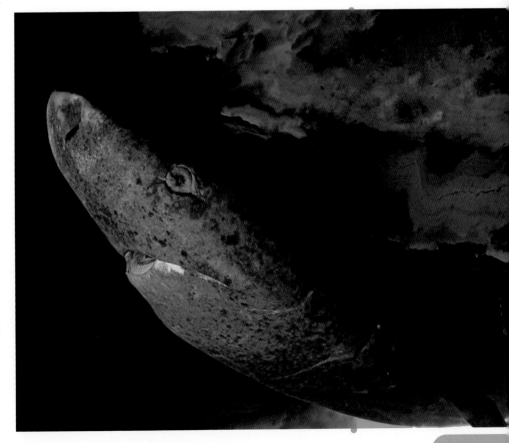

Bite and Roll
Greenland sharks use their pointed top teeth to hold prey. Then, they roll their head to slice out a chunk of flesh with their bottom teeth. They leave a round bite wound on larger prey.

Sleeper Sharks
Greenland sharks are in a group called "sleeper" sharks because of their slow movement through cold, deep waters.

Often described as the world's slowest shark, this rarely seen fish swims at a relaxed pace. It might take 30 seconds to move its tail from one side to the other. But speed isn't everything, and studies show that Greenland sharks might be faster than originally thought, swimming with short bursts of speed. Scientists have reportedly

been startled by large Greenland sharks sneaking up or stalking them to the water's surface, like the sharks would a seal. Fortunately, while the sharks got very close, they only watched the scientists.

Their diet mostly consists of faster moving prey. Younger or smaller Greenland sharks eat squid. Older and larger sharks eat fish and seals.

Land Food
Greenland sharks even eat land animals—such as reindeer, moose, and polar bears—that walk close to the water's edge or fall in.

Greenland sharks live in water that's below freezing! Special chemicals in their blood work like antifreeze. The chemicals keep the sharks from freezing and also make these sharks toxic to eat.

Blinded
Greenland sharks often have parasites attached to one or both eyes, which makes the sharks partially or completely blind. This doesn't seem to bother the sharks, though. They rely on their other senses in the deep, dark sea.

Mature Moms
Females are not able to have babies until they are 150 years old.

Greenland sharks spend most of their time at depths of 1,312 to 2,297 feet (400 to 700 m). But they may cruise even deeper. In 1988, a 20-foot (6-m)-long male was seen 1.4 miles (2.2 km) down near an old shipwreck.

Greenland sharks live at least 250 years, though some may be more than 500 years old. That means the shark near the shipwreck could have been there when the ship sank more than 160 years ago!

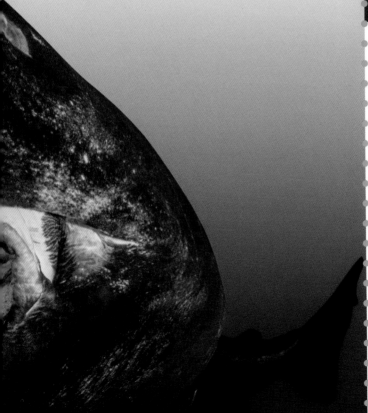

What Stinks So Good? Greenland sharks swim toward stinky smells. Like other sharks, they are scavengers, which means they eat dead animals.

Sperm Whale Greenland sharks can be prey for an even larger apex predator: the sperm whale. The whale might go after the shark's large, fat-filled liver. But the whale has to get through the shark's sharp skin scales first.

BASKING SHARK

Open mouth. Swim. Let food float in. Repeat. The basking shark slowly swims with its enormous mouth wide open.

Special bristles in the shark's gills trap tiny food. To feed, these sharks swim with their mouths open, closing their jaws every 30 to 60 seconds. After collecting water, gill rakers filter the water through five large gills, capturing plankton. Basking sharks filter an average of 1,585 gallons (6,000 L) of water per hour. After about 30 seconds, the shark closes its mouth. Then, it opens its mouth and begins the feeding process all over again.

Great Big Gills
Most sharks have small gills on the sides of their heads. A basking shark's giant gills circle almost its entire head.

Big Babies
A newborn basking shark is five to six feet (1.5 to 1.8 m) long. That's the size of a human adult.

Basking sharks earn their apex predator status through size alone. This massive shark is the second-largest shark—and fish—in the world. Large basking sharks can reach the length of a school bus! Their size and weight prevent most, if any, predators from hunting them.

Leaping Sharks
Basking sharks breach, or jump out of the water. They might breach to communicate with other basking sharks.

Filter-Feeders
Basking sharks, whale sharks, and megamouth sharks are the only three species of sharks that filter feed. But unlike whale and megamouth sharks, which actively suck in water, basking sharks just wait for food to float in.

Basking sharks got their name because they bask, or lie, in the sun on the water's surface. But these sun lovers also spend months in the deep sea, down to 3,000 feet (900 m).

These sharks are huge, but their food is not. Basking sharks filter plankton smaller than a grain of rice. Plankton include tiny plants, animals, and eggs. To fill its belly, a

Copepods
Basking sharks eat tiny shrimp-like animals called copepods. They can be smaller than an ant.

copepod

Staying Separate
Male and female basking sharks live and hunt in different places.

basking shark filters 2,000 tons (1,814 t) of water an hour. That's about the amount of water in a swimming pool.

A large basking shark's liver can weigh 2,500 pounds (1,134 kg)! The liver stores oil, which provides energy when food is unavailable or during long migrations when the shark does not hunt. The liver also helps the shark float.

Staggering Stats

A basking shark's mouth can be more than three feet (1 m) wide. That's about the size of a Hula-Hoop! Its tongue can be more than two feet (0.8 m) long, which is about the length of a skateboard. And its dorsal fin can be more than six feet (2 m) tall.

Elephant Seal Size
A male elephant seal is the length and weight of a car. Females are much smaller.

Molting
Elephant seals, harbor seals, and California sea lions also come onshore to molt. Molting is when they shed their old fur and new fur grows in.

GREAT WHITE SHARK

Just off the coast, the great white shark waits. It finds the perfect spot to hide in the shadows. The hungry shark listens, smells, and watches for elephant seals. A seal slides below the waves. It swims a short way before the great white launches upward from below. This apex predator delivers what might be a deadly bite from behind. The wounded seal keeps swimming. The shark waits for the seal to become weak. Then, the shark slices chunks of meat with its rows of sharp teeth and swallows them whole.

In the winter, during the seal and sea lion pupping season, great whites hunt along the West Coast of North America from Mexico to Alaska, USA. The seals and sea lions come onshore to have their pups. Great whites wait for seals and sea lions as they enter the water to find food. When pupping season is over, the seals and sea lions head out to sea in different directions. The sharks leave, too.

Fueled by Fat
The elephant seal's thick layer of fat provides a lot of calories. Sharks store this energy in their livers. The energy fuels the sharks' long-distance migrations when they do not eat.

Sniffing the Air
Great white sharks stick their head out of the water to look around and pick up scents from the air.

Satellite Tags
Many tags send signals to satellites that track sharks' movements and locations. Scientists download and analyze the data.

Temporary Tags
The tags are designed to fall off the shark after a certain amount of time. Scientists collect the equipment from the ocean's surface.

Great whites are one of the most studied shark species, yet we know so little about them. Inventing and using technology to study great whites and other sharks is essential to understanding and protecting them, their prey, and their habitats. Scientists use underwater robots called autonomous underwater vehicles (AUVs) to safely follow and video sharks. Because the AUVs can "swim" with the sharks, they can provide invaluable insight into the shark's world without disrupting the shark's behavior. And there's another advantage. The AUVs can handle the bumps and bites of great whites better than human divers can!

Reputation aside, a great white's attempts to catch prey are not always successful. They fail, and often. Scars on prey show that many animals somehow escape after getting bitten by these sharks. AUV videos have captured such hunting misses. In one video, a great white stalks a sea turtle, swimming behind it. But when the sea turtle notices, it races away unharmed. In another video, a great white loses out when an agile sea lion quickly swims circles around the predator and then disappears.

Apex vs. Apex
Orcas, or killer whales, are also apex predators. Great whites leave when orcas show up at seal and sea lion rookeries, or breeding colonies. Sometimes, the sharks move a safe distance away and wait. Other times, the sharks leave to find another rookery for the rest of the season.

Breaching
Great white sharks sometimes jump out of the water to catch prey.

For a long time, it was assumed that most sharks, especially great whites, were solitary creatures. But recent studies of great whites and other sharks suggest a very different story.

Scientists used different kinds of technology to create a "social tagging" study to find out more about how sharks interact. This technology included an AUV and electronic and acoustic tags.

Electronic tags tracked where and how fast the sharks swam and when they turned or dove. These tags also tracked information such as water temperature. The social tags tracked when the sharks got near other tagged sharks.

The social tags revealed that great whites might swim and eat together more often than originally thought. While some sharks kept their distance, other sharks often swam within 100 feet (30 m) of each other. Two in particular seemed very social, interacting with many different individuals and sometimes swimming with other sharks for more than an hour. Scientists think this social behavior may be a way to share some kind of information.

The sharks did not hunt together, but they peacefully moved in the same locations and directions. It was kind of like people in a grocery store, looking for food in the same place.

Shark Feast
Video footage documented great whites taking turns sharing the remains of a large whale.

Changes in Diet
Like other sharks, a great white's diet changes as it grows. Younger sharks hunt smaller prey. Older sharks hunt larger marine mammals, such as seals, sea lions, and dolphins, as well as large squid and fish.

Nickname
A great white shark is also called a white pointer.

Technology has also shown that some great white sharks spend time in unexpected habitats, including deeper water.

Every fall, great whites return to Guadalupe Island, Mexico, to hunt seals and sea lions. Scientists have been observing how white sharks hunt in shallow water for years.

But what—and where—else do the sharks hunt? Adult and subadult male great whites arrive months before elephant seals. Researchers used an AUV to follow, observe, and video the male sharks. The footage shows that the sharks dive to the twilight zone: the deep sea, where sunlight

has faded and the ocean is dark. There, the great whites hunt large squid, such as the neon flying squid, jumbo squid, and giant squid.

Scars on the sharks' heads and bodies from the squid's sharp suckers show that the squid do not give in to this apex predator easily.

Jumbo Squid Suckers
Giant squid have sharp tooth-like structures around the outside of their suckers. They use them to hold on to prey and fight off predators.

Hiding Spot
Scientists thought that great whites didn't enter or hunt in kelp forests. But small cameras attached to great whites off the coast of South Africa showed the sharks hiding in the seaweed, possibly to hunt young seals.

Tech in Motion
Scientists have used uncrewed surface vehicles (USVs) to study great whites traveling to the Café. The vehicles travel long distances on the water's surface using wind and solar power. They transmit information from the shark's tracking devices to satellites.

Finding Friends
South African great whites and those found in Western Australia cross the Indian Ocean to interact.

Another discovery took scientists by surprise. After pupping season, great whites leave the Pacific Coast of North America and head west. Meanwhile, great white sharks in Hawaii, USA, head east. They meet in the Pacific Ocean, somewhere between Hawaii and Mexico, in a place scientists call the White Shark Café.

The White Shark Café is about the size of New Mexico, USA. While there, the sharks spend a lot of time in deeper, darker water. Scientists discovered that great whtes travel here to hunt.

Are there other cafés out there? No one knows. Around the world, adult white sharks leave coastal areas, and where they go is still a mystery.

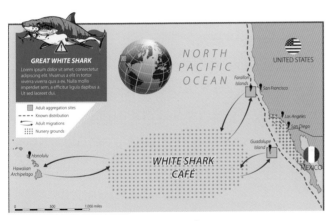

White Shark Café tracking map from California, Mexico, and Hawaii

Long-Distance Swimmer
One tagged great white nicknamed Nicole was tracked swimming 6,200 miles (11,000 km) from South Africa to Australia and back.

Keep on Tracking
A large-scale tracking program in Australia has tagged more than 250 sharks with satellite and acoustic tags since the year 2000.

Seafood
Sharks and other fish are an important part of many people's diet.

APEX, BUT NOT INVINCIBLE

Great whites and other sharks may be at the top of the food web, but they are still vulnerable. Many sharks are threatened and endangered because of overfishing, habitat destruction, and other human-caused challenges.

This makes humans the most dangerous and deadly apex predator.

For example, humans kill about 20 million blue sharks every year. That means blue sharks are the most overfished shark in the world.

Great hammerhead sharks are endangered. People accidently catch hammerheads in nets that are set for other types of fish. People also intentionally hunt hammerhead sharks for their fins for shark fin soup.

All of this overfishing has caused a severe drop in the hammerhead shark population. The decline is as high as 90 percent in some places.

Basking sharks have few natural predators. Humans are their worst enemy. During the last century, people hunted basking sharks to near extinction in some parts of the world. People mistakenly thought the sharks were eating some of the same fish they were eating, creating competition.

Today, many countries protect basking sharks. Citizen science groups and fishers help by reporting sightings of the sharks to scientists. Biologists use this information to track populations and locations of basking sharks. In some places, like the North Atlantic Ocean, basking shark populations are starting to slowly grow.

Overhunting Sharks
Because overhunting sharks, sometimes only for their large fins, has reduced populations to dangerously low levels, many countries have made buying and selling shark fins illegal.

Declining Numbers
The shortfin mako shark population has declined almost 80 percent in the North Atlantic Ocean, possibly due to overfishing.

Shark Nursery
Many sharks give birth near shore and in protected bays. These shallow-water nurseries provide protection from larger predators. Protecting the nurseries helps protect sharks.

Sharks that are apex predators are essential to their ecosystems. Here's an example of how.

Sea turtle numbers are growing, thanks to strong efforts to save these threatened reptiles. But unfortunately, in some of those same locations, sharks have been overhunted. The sea turtle's main predator is then not there, enabling the large reptiles to overeat the seagrass. Seagrass is an important home and food for many animals. It also plays an essential role in the health of our planet. The meadows take up carbon dioxide, which helps control the climate.

Understanding the role of apex predators like sharks is important. The information gives scientists a better picture of how an ecosystem works. It shows them how animals interact and live in a particular habitat. It helps them understand predator-prey relationships. This information is crucial in protecting species and their habitats. When we protect apex predators, we protect entire ecosystems.

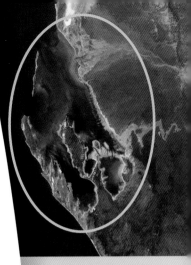

Seagrass from Space
Different kinds of seagrass are found all over the world, from warm waters to the freezing Arctic Ocean. Some meadows are big enough to see from space!

APEX SHARKS SHOWCASE

TIGER SHARK
Size: 10 to 14 feet (3 to 4.3 m) long; maximum 18 feet (5.5 m) long
Life span: 20 to 27 years, possibly up to 50 years

BULL SHARK
Size: 5.9 to 7.4 feet (1.8 to 2.3 m) long; maximum 12 feet (3.7 m) long
Life span: up to 32 years

SHORTFIN MAKO SHARK
Size: females 9 feet (2.7 m) long; males 7 feet (2 m) long
Life span: 30 years

HAMMERHEAD SHARK
Size: 6.8 to 9.8 feet (2 to 3 m) long; maximum 18.4 to 20 feet (5.6 to 6 m) long
Life span: up to 30 years

GREENLAND SHARK
Size: 8 to 15 feet (2.4 to 4.6 m)
long; maximum 24 feet (7.3 m) long
Life span: at least 270 years,
possibly up to 500 years

BASKING SHARK
Size: up to 40 feet (12 m) long
Life span: up to 30 years

GREAT WHITE SHARK
Size: 16.4 feet (5 m) long; maximum
21 feet (6.4 m) long
Life span: up to 70 years

GLOSSARY

Ampullae of Lorenzini
[am-POOL-ah of lor-un-ZEE-nee]
Sensory pits on a shark's head and
snout that detect electrical currents

Cold-blooded
An animal that cannot make its own
heat and is the same temperature as
its surroundings

Ecosystem
Interactions between plants,
animals, and the environment
where they live

Endangered
An animal population that is at risk
of dying out

Fins
Used by sharks to swim, turn, and
stop, and for stability and balance

Gills
Used by sharks to breathe

Habitat
A place where an animal lives

Overfishing
Removing fish or ocean animals
faster than animals can reproduce
in order to maintain a healthy
population

Population
The same kinds of animals that live,
travel, or reproduce in the same area

Predator
An animal that eats other animals

Prey
Animals that predators eat

Rookery
A breeding colony, such as of seals
or sea lions

Satellite
A spacecraft that orbits Earth to
gather information

Seagrass
A kind of plant that grows in
shallow seawater; it has roots and
gets its energy from the sun.

Seaweed
A kind of algae; it gets its energy
from the sun but does not have
roots.

Twilight zone
The ocean depth between 600 to
3,300 feet (200 to 1,000 m)

Warm-blooded
An animal that can produce its own
body heat, regardless of the
temperature around it

INDEX

QUIZ

Answer the questions to see what you have learned. Check your answers in the key below.

1. Which shark lives hundreds of years?

2. Which shark swims up rivers?

3. True or False: Female sharks feed newborn shark pups.

4. How did basking sharks get their name?

5. How does a hammerhead find its food?

6. Which is the fastest shark?

7. What can happen without the presence of apex predators?

8. What do tiger sharks do if their prey sees them?

1. Greenland shark 2. Bull shark 3. False 4. They bask, or lie, in the sun on the water's surface 5. It uses its ampullae of Lorenzini to sense prey under the sand 6. Shortfin mako shark 7. The entire food web can be disrupted or even destroyed 8. They stop the hunt and look for other prey